Holiday Coloring Fun

Illustrated by Molly Harrison

Featuring angels, polar bears, fairies and more,
this coloring book contains twenty one images ranging
from simple to more complex,
and is meant for adults and older children.

For more information about the artist, please visit

www.mollyharrisonart.com